# Unfree Associations

# UNFREE ASSOCIATIONS

MICHAEL COVINO

Berkeley Poets Workshop & Press
Berkeley, California
1982

Acknowledgments:
Some of these poems have appeared in the following magazines: *Antenna, Berkeley Poets Cooperative, Invisible City, The Journal of Popular Film and Television, Kayak, Mickle Street Review, Mississippi Mud, Partisan Review, Pig Iron, Poetry Now,* and *San Fernando Poetry Journal.*

"Autumn Leaves" and "Prescribed Form" appeared in *Poetry.*

Cover by Anthony Dubovsky

Photo of author by George Csicsery



ISBN 0-917658-17-5

Berkeley Poets Workshop & Press
P.O. Box 459
Berkeley, California 94701

Typeset by Ampersand Typography, Berkeley, California.
Printed by Braun-Brumfield, Inc., Ann Arbor, Michigan.

CONTENTS

*While some quietly drowned or hanged themselves, the others proudly stalked the land, brooding upon new horrors.*

Franz Innerhofer, *Beautiful Days*

# Unfree Associations

THE LEGACY

1.

When in 1848 I led a lobster on a satin leash through the throngs
  of merchants and aristocrats at the opera on opening night—
When in 1857 I dyed my hair green, then mounted the lectern
  and screamed, "Hypocrite listener!—You!—My twin!—My
  brother!—"
When in 1871 I, age sixteen, climbed the barricades of the Paris
  Commune, and at seventeen ran off with the leading poet of
  my day whom I replaced as the leading poet of my day—
When in 1915 I strode through Moscow in a top hat with a
  gold-topped cane shouting my monstrous verses through a
  megaphone—
When in 1922 I attended mass in the Vatican with a blood
  capsule in my mouth and just as the wafer was placed between
  my lips bit down hard on the capsule—
When in 1939 I dressed in leather and rode my motorcycle
  roaring into the South American writer's funeral procession—
When in 1956 I threw potato salad from a New York delicatessen
  in the faces of the university lecturers on Dadaism—
When in 1966 I said, "Here's a poem," then addressed my
  courteous Frankfurt audience with, "You scumbags. You
  sappy cunts. You barbaric pricks. You plain old fucking
  assholes—"

When I did all these things—
When I did all these things and more—
Yes, when I did all these things
    they threw me out
        but also showered me with dinner invitations—
    called me an anti-Christ
        but also "the one true Christian in the house—"
    said, "What nerve—the upstart!"
        but also, "What a clever way to promote his new
            book!—

denounced me as an anarchist
but also, "How delightful, he's a communist—"
expressed shock / disgust / outrage / boredom
but also beamed with pleasure
but also beamed with pleasure—

And when I presented them with the hard evidence of their collective ownership of the contradiction the unilateral cancellation the veneration of the art the something-else-again the life—

When I grabbed them by the shoulders and shook them—

It was no use, and
I wandered off in a stupor,

exhausted—

2.

When I announced I was tired of literature—
When I went into exile—
When I passed the hat and said not money *blood*—
When I quit writing to join the International Brigade—
When I flaunted my homosexuality in the beer cellars of Munich—
When I issued a fiery manifesto from Mexico—
When I said not art but politics—
When I said not politics but art—
When I returned from exile on my return ticket—
When I spoke in a voice that cut through all layers of society—
When I spoke in a voice that incurred the wrath of the bourgeoisie without creating a working-class public in compensation—
When I exposed my genitals in a crowded room—
When I exposed my brains in a room crowded with genitals—
When I lapsed into a quarter-century silence—
When I lapsed into a quarter-century silence while collecting thirty thousand a year on retainer from a New York publisher—

When I spoke in the dialect of my countrymen—
When I spoke in the dialect of my parents' kitchen help—
When I kicked the bourgeoisie in the ass—
When I walked on all fours before the bourgeoisie—
When I spoke from the poor naked shivering heart—
When I spoke in the first person, confessional-private, "This-is-me-but-not-quite-me" with a wink of the old eye—
When I drank myself from poem to poem—
When I drank myself, first slowly, then more quickly, to death—
When I blew my brains out with a revolver—
When I was thrown before a Fascist firing squad and shot dead—
When I drowned myself—
When I went underground with the French resistance—
When I broadcast over the Fascist radio—
When I stuck my head in an oven—
When I was stuck in an oven—
When I died shattered and hopeless in New York City—
When I leaped horribly to my death—
When I was left to rot in a madhouse—
When I was worked to death like a slave in Vladivostok—
When I died of cancer in a Chilean military ward and named the cancer the United States—
When I spoke in the world-historical—
When I spoke to express myself—
When I spoke to evict myself—
When I—

3.

cried out

cried out

cried out

## LANDSCAPE

"Hello . . . ? Is anybody home?"
*The Texas Chainsaw Massacre*

It's been so long. You're driving through the countryside, the morning air is cold and bright. But out across the low-lying fields, the ground fog clings to the legs of the billboard.

As the day wears on, you whisper, "Like in a dream, everything's just like it used to be." But already one's thoughts are turning away.

In the rearview mirror: someone in a long, dark coat is walking along the edge of the road. And the old familiar feeling of traveling through a strange country is taking hold.

The car glides through the park at dusk, and the woods creak all around. If anyone's in there, they remain hidden.

Just as the car reaches the blinking red traffic light, the rain starts gently falling.

And though the cool wet air still feels pleasant enough, the maples have already begun to go red—

:and the storm clouds break apart in great, slow motions—

:the last light seems strangely flattened and compressed—

:and through the drizzle, across the valley, a car climbs the distant slope and disappears over the far ridge.

## NOMENCLATURE

"They used to call Joe Barboza 'The Animal.'
That's because he was an animal."

*but*

Not a clue to:

who
*slashed*
Charlie the Blade

who
*impaled*
Icepick Barney

who
*dismembered*
Three-Finger Brown

who
*starved*
Fat Al

who
*axed*
Vito the Chopper

who
*chloroformed*
The Doctor

who
*silenced*
Mike the Wiseguy

who
*throttled*
The Clutching Hand

who
*shot*
Frankie Shots

who
*drowned*
Sam the Plumber

who
*strangled*
Jimmy the Giraffe

who
*electrocuted*
Jimmy Blue Eyes

who
*butchered*
Ronnie the Pig

who
*choked*
Joe Yak

*yet*

Years later
The Animal recalled:

"The day of the burial it was snowing so hard
even The Boot kept sinking in to his knees."

"It was cold."

"The pine trees sparkled with frost . . ."

## FALSE PHRASES

When the world is reduced to a cold, bright morning,—a beach for two faithful children,—a potato in all its earthy holiness,—a single note of song,—we shall have vanished.

. . .

My father's childhood home, white clapboard house, small town New England,—the potatoes pushing up in the back garden,—the mailman whistling down the leafy street,—and look!—"That diesel pulling the long line of flatcars . . . *Maine!* . . . *Pacific!* . . . See how the engineer waves to me!"
*Late October, the gypsy girl and I,—we walked barefoot down a Nova Scotian beach at dusk,—she dipped her hand into a tidal pool and withdrew a perfect seashell,—we cooked periwinkles over an open fire that night,—and slept beneath the stars,—*

. . .

And even if it should be true,—
still,—
on a cold, clear morning
the last coal goes out
and the words begin to draw back from the observation,
altering forever the nature of the observed.

. . .

QUESTIONS:

What was the tune the mailman whistled? No tune, nothing at all, he was shy and had a harelip.
But then what about the leafy street, what about—? And up and down the leafy street, massacres and mergers are being hatched.

But did the seashell not sound like the ocean? Did the—?

No, a jet was climbing in the dusk,—
a slimy sandcrab lowered itself from the shell into your ear,—
and two faithful children—O come on now!—are never faithful,—
and anyway you were alone,—
and anyway you never got that far north,—
and anyway—well, you get the picture.

But the words? the phrases? the—?
Shoddy salesmen working on commission,—you should never have said, "Come in," but *"Keep moving."*
But the dreams! the dreams!
And even the nature of our dreams has changed.

But then what about the potatoes pushing up in the earth?
What about the white clapboard house?
For far behind the auto body shop the distant fields lie fallow,—
And on the railroad siding beneath the shade trees the potatoes are rotting (at an undisclosed price) in heaps on the unattended flatcars,—
And the white clapboard house is exploding into a thousand cities twinkling on the edge of this changing night.

## IN POINT OF FACT

1.

(The American Indians strained the perseverance of the missionaries who wanted to teach them how to read.)

2.

(The caravan of jet black Citroëns carrying the Parisian poets parked in the circular drive in front of the chalet.)

3.

(Having inherited his grandmother's fortune, he was free to pursue a literary career without worrying about earning a living.)

4.

(Flaunting his Nobel Prize everywhere he went, Norman quickly acquired a reputation for conceit.)

5.

(Before the Russian Revolution, many aristocratic poets did not know about the living conditions of the poor, or knew and did not care.)

6.

(The caravan of gray Mercedes 600s carrying the Bavarian poets parked in the circular drive in front of the castle.)

7.

(Never particularly respectful of convention, Allen Ginsberg refused to wear a tuxedo to his sister's wedding.)

8.

(Because W.S. Merwin will always be looked upon as a controversial writer, critical debate about his work will continue for years to come.)

9.

(A long poem like *The Odyssey* can be made into a movie more easily than an idea like John Keats' "negative capability," which is probably more suitable for a slide-show discussion.)

10.

(The caravan of pure white Silver Cloud Rolls Royces carrying the American poets parked in the circular drive in front of the Texan's country manor, and the American poets stepped out—)

## PRESCRIBED FORM

Since this is the way such things are usually done, the killer leaves a fifteen per cent tip with his dinner.
Pretending to be perfectly normal, the safecracker stops to check the racing results.
Solely for the sake of appearance, the white collar criminal straightens the knot in his tie.
Under the guise of conventional behavior, the rapist stoops to tie his shoe.
Behind the facade of everyday normality, the kidnaper purchases a balloon from the park vendor.

Every day, every hour, every moment—
Morning, noon, and night—
On and on—
Without stopping—

A crook is behaving according to protocol—
A thug is standing on ceremony—
A strangler is heeding the social graces—
A thief is doing the only decent thing—
A gangster says, "Excuse me—"

For years on end—
Day after day—
Hour after hour—

A hit man has taken out the garbage—
A felon has not left the screen door ajar—
A mobster has jiggled the toilet handle—
A hoodlum has defrosted the refrigerator—

Again and again—
Over and over—

Since this is the way such things are usually done: someone is doing it again as usual.

## WHAT IS YOUR NAME?

Are you proud of your name? Are you ashamed of your name? Do you wish you had a different name? What would you like your name to be?

*"Put your John Hancock right here!"*

Do they get your name mixed up with others? Is it a Christian name? Is it a common name? Is it an unusual name? Is your name in the social register? Is it an ethnic name?

*"Put your John Hancock right here!"*

What is your assumed name? What alias do you travel under? What is your pen name? What is your pseudonym? What name do you sneak around under after dark?

*"Put your John Hancock right here!"*

What is your title? What does it say on your door? What do you wish it said on your door? Do you sometimes think of yourself as a number rather than as a name? What is your label? What is your tag? Do you have a good name? Do you have a reputable name? Do you have a name that insures quality? Is your name *worth money?*

*"Put your John Hancock right here!"*

What would you like your name to be? Do you wish you were called Albert Schweitzer? What about Charlie Chaplin? How about Pablo Picasso? Then again Mark Twain? Bertrand Russell? Madame Curie? Albert Einstein? Leo Tolstoy? Wouldn't it be nice if your name was Rockefeller, or Vanderbilt, or Morgan? If your name was a name to open doors? *Is* your name Rockefeller, or Vanderbilt, or Morgan? At parties do you drop names? Do you do this because you are insecure and does your insecurity stem from the simple fact that your own name isn't worth dropping? When you are introduced to famous people do you mumble, "I'm nobody," and smile shyly?

*"Put your John Hancock right here!"*

What names make you uneasy? What names fill you with dread? Have you read *The Unnamable?* Are you ashamed of your ethnic name? Have you had your name changed legally? Are you glad at least your name's not Goering? Are you happy you're not called Charles Starkweather? That you don't respond to the name Richard Speck? What about Benedict Arnold? How about Richard Nixon? Quisling? Brutus? Lee Harvey Oswald? Would it be hard to live with the name Judas Iscariot? Suppose your name was Pablo Picasso but not *that* Pablo Picasso? Would you then have your name changed legally to avoid embarrassment every time you filled out a job application? When you were little were you ever beat up by tough Irish kids who refused to believe you were half-Irish because your last name didn't start with *o* but ended with *o*? Have you ever tried chanting your name for so long that it turns into sounds, simply sounds, merely sounds, nothing but strings of nonsensical sounds that have absolutely nothing to do with who you are? Who are you?

*"Put your John Hancock right here!"*

What name do you use when you forge traveler's checks? What name do you scream under interrogation in the torture chamber? What is the name they force you to sign to the list of false confessions? What pseudonym do you use in the underground resistance paper? Do you worry that their secret police have teams of literary critics whose job it is to determine by means of stylistic comparisons the authorship of these pseudonymous articles?

*"Put your John Hancock right here!"*

What is your pen name? What is your real name? What is your proper name? *Did* your great-great grandfather put his John Hancock on the Declaration of Independence? We didn't think so. What is your first name? What is your given name? *What name will they take away from you?*

## IN THE POSTWAR PERIOD

1.

The cold north winds
howled through the housing projects
clustered like giants on the edges of the city
—looming, glimmering—in the vast raw night
as we warmed our feet in the lobbies
in the postwar period

2.

In the early years
the Housing Authority
put Christmas trees in the lobbies

We smashed the ornaments
and lit the branches
then danced around the trees

3.

In the blue shadows of the apartment towers
we'd pull the fire alarms

then watch the engines
streak through the streets

4.

*In the postwar period*
*In the postwar period*
We linked our arms and ran through the projects
waking everyone up
*In the postwar period*
*In the postwar period* we sang
in the incredible postwar period

5.

In the freezing shadows of the new landscape—
In the cinder block stairwells—
In the piss-stink elevators—
On the frozen gravelly roofs—

But fucking was impossible
in the postwar period

6.

In stolen cars we'd approach the intersections
where officers helped the blind across
then hit the accelerators
slamming into them
The years were too funny for words

7.

In the frosted blue glow
*of the corner street lamps—*

In the freezing shadows
*of the new world architecture—*

Stretching across
*the unrelenting landscape—*

:as we howled on the edges of the city

## CONTAMINATION

He could hear the waves slapping against the hulls of the yachts tied up to the dock just below the restaurant's sheltered terrace—

Two large white dogs with russet spots lay on the thick rug next to the fireplace whose burning logs crackled in the silence—

He glanced up from the menu at the sound of mules banging on the black tiles of the long hallway—

The key made a resounding click as she dropped it onto the black marble tabletop—

The waiter came and spread the white tablecloth, then poured a coffee so rich and black that the aroma stung the nostrils—

As she drank the coffee her elbow stuck to the glossy surface of the photograph which he had slid across the table—

*Watch out!*

The sticky black dregs at the bottom of the cup—

The wet red leaves splattered against the window—

The two white dogs with russet spots—

The crackling of logs—

The banging on tiles—

The click on marble—

*Watch out!*

She clapped her hand to her mouth in horror as she watched the brown stain spreading on the white linen tablecloth while the waiter approached angrily from the other side of the restaurant and the two white dogs with russet spots leaped to their feet, tugging at their long chains and barking horribly.

ETHIOPIA SALUTING THE COLORS

1. General Motors (Detroit)
   $54,961,300,000
2. Exxon (New York)
   $54,126,219,000
3. Ford Motor (Dearborn, Mich.)
   $37,841,500,000
4. Mobil (New York)
   $32,125,828,000
5. Texaco (White Plains, N.Y.)
   $27,920,499,000

---

6. Standard Oil of California (San Francisco)
   $20,917,331,000
7. International Business Machines (Armonk, N.Y.)
   $18,133,184,000
8. Gulf Oil (Pittsburgh)
   $17,840,000,000
9. General Electric (Fairfield, Conn.)
   $17,518,600,000
10. Chrysler (Highland Park, Mich.)
   $16,708,300,000

---

## MOVIE STARS IN THEIR EVERYDAY LIVES

Who should walk into the ice cream parlor with ***137 FLAVORS*** but Humphrey Bogart! Slouching forward, the countergirl says huskily, "If you need anything, don't whistle. Just take a number and wait on line. You know how to—" "Double scoop," Bogart snaps. "Gorilla Vanilla. Whipped Rum Papaya." "All out," she growls, but then drops her voice to a throaty whisper, "though we do have Blow Out The Cantaloupe."

A young blonde carrying a Polaroid, her moist lips parted, her blue eyes wide with innocent wonder, in blue jeans so incredibly tight-fitting that they capture the world-imagination, asks in a breathy voice, "May ah-I-I take your picture?"

Suddenly there's a crash of glass—a motorcycle hurtles through the window. Marlon Brando climbs off, smiles broadly, grunts and orders a Jungle Banana, and, pointing to the pet with jangled nerves on his shoulder, says, "Get my monkey fucked."

Just then Marilyn screams, dropping her Polaroid with a crash to the floor. Mickey Mouse is soft-shoe dancing under the tables!

*Whereupon* John Wayne drops through the skylight, reaches for his Colt, and blasts the mouse—

*Whereupon* James Cagney, Edward G. Robinson, and George Raft burst, sneering, through the front door and open fire on the mouse with an incredible clatter of tommy guns—

*Whereupon,* or almost whereupon, King Kong, who two blocks back overheard the order for Gorilla Vanilla, who one block back overheard the order for a single fucked monkey, walks through the wall and crushes what's left of the mouse in his fist, but then—he spots Marilyn of the haunting blond hair—lets the mouse slip through his fist.

Face impassive, eyes slightly narrowed beneath the brim of his cowboy hat, chewing thoughtfully on his stubby cigar, Clint Eastwood sizes up the situation, carefully flips his serape over his left shoulder, then leaves the line, lifts the mouse by its flat black tail, drops it into the trash basket through the hinged door that says THANK YOU, and turns and relights his cigar.

Meanwhile Marlene Dietrich, finishing a thick hot fudge sundae, watching Kong who's watching Marilyn, licks her fingers and smacks her lips, then eases up behind Kong and runs her fingers through Kong's soft silky hair while attaching a velvet leash to his collar.

In all the commotion no one has noticed the chubby man with dignified carriage and triple chin who has unobtrusively / inconspicuously / unassumingly / almost invisibly / walked in and, without ceremony, ordered a vanilla cone and left.

So many movie stars in one ice cream shop!

Suddenly everyone turns. A little man with a derby and a mustache has just appeared in the doorway. With a hitch of his baggy trousers, he waddles in on roller skates and darts a look of helpless awe at the endless rows of ice creams. Faced with such abundance, he can't make up his mind even though he is hungry. Actually, he is incredibly hungry since he is also penniless and hasn't eaten for days.

The little man points to one. His mind changes. He points to another—shakes his head again. Another—again shakes his head. And another—*again.* Another—*again.* Another—

Bacall, exasperated, raises her hand. She takes a cone and puts on one scoop, she adds a second, then a third, and a fourth, and a fifth, a sixth, a seventh—she's working her way methodically down the row while the little man, trembling, watches in utter disbelief as the ice cream mounts toward the ceiling.

Yet he is hungry. She hands the cone to the little man and it begins to lean—he skates one way. It leans the other way—he skates back. Now this way . . . now that . . . *backwards* . . . *forwards* . . .

The little man is skating rings, darting bites and licks at the cone, tripping, slipping, regaining his balance, miraculously never quite crashing.

The tears of laughter in all the stars' eyes have stopped. The little man is whirling faster and faster. Marilyn is trying desperately to put her camera back together. Brando, the picture of thoughtfulness, has ceased rolling the chewing gum in his mouth. Even Bogart and Eastwood keep nodding and going, each in his own way, "Heh."

For two or three seconds everyone is actually happy.

Suddenly John Wayne shouts, "He didn't pay," and reaches for his holster.

A gentle hand restrains him. It is Marlon Brando—the gray-haired Marlon Brando! With courtly reserve, his frail frame clothed in an unassuming three-piece suit and tie, flanked by his *caporegimes,* he says, "Please. Let the little man continue."

Wayne looks down at the hand that is touching his own and narrows his eyes. "I'm afraid the fellah is still gonna hafta pay the lady," he says in a soft but insistent drawl, and takes two steps backward.

"Come," Brando says blandly, taking out a bankroll and counting off the notes. "We are reasonable men. I would like to engage the services of the little man for a friend's club." (The younger Brando, his leather jacket unzipped, sitting astride his motorcycle, has been watching this performance in a trance.)

Yet it is too late. The sun is going down. The little man with the bowler and mustache hands the king-size cone to a startled Kong, and before anyone can stop him skates out the door, heading off down the empty road, alone once more, his little tramp's figure growing smaller and smaller until all that one can see is a mere dot at the vanishing point where the long straight road converges on the horizon.

## EXTINCTION

in
the
jungles
the
natives
ambush
the
tax
collectors

&

The Death Merchant
battles
the
Castro
cruds
along
the
Prado
where
in
happier
days
whores
and
an
estimated
5000
beggars
roamed
freely
beneath
the swaying laurels

&

"a lot of the old flavor was missing"

&

on
TV
the
crazy
yet
likable
escapee
who
holds
the
pretty
secretary
hostage
in
her
boss's
barricaded
office
asks
the
coppers
to
slide
a
pizza
under
the
door

&

The Executioner
wipes
out
the
Mafia
in
New York
&
Chicago
&
Las Vegas
&
the Caribbean
&
California
&
Boston
&
San Diego
&
Sicily
&
Texas
&
Hawaii
&
St. Louis
&
Canada
&
Colorado

&

the
real-life

thrill
killer
before
strangling
the
eleven
innocent
student
nurses
to
death
with
a
black
silk
stocking
allows
them
each
three
last
telephone
calls
to
relatives
and
close friends

&

"At one time . . ."

"a double-line of coconut palms"

## SPORTS EVENT

Then again, during the last inning
of the last game
of the most nerve-racking game of them all
when the broadcaster saw
the sky darkening to the north
behind the bleachers filled with poor people
and said, "The dark, ominous crowds—"

## TELEVISION PARTICIPATES IN THE PROJECT OF REDRESSING HISTORICAL IMBALANCES IN THE AREA OF RACE RELATIONS

*Monday—*
The exploitation of an Eskimo college quarterback has Felix fuming.

*Tuesday—*
A Puerto Rican fence helps Paul retrieve a stolen watch.

*Wednesday—*
A special report on Algerians who have come to France looking for the good life. But what many have found is grueling manual labor or unemployment, unacceptance by the French, and loneliness.

*Thursday—*
While Archie campaigns to keep a black family out of the neighborhood, Edith accepts a dinner invitation from the Jeffersons. Archie is hopping mad.

*Friday—*
A Negro soldier, unjustly convicted of murder, escapes and is sought by the man who trusted him.

*Saturday—*
A down-on-her-luck divorcee struggling to make ends meet comes home one night from a date and encounters a Hispanic teen-ager slashing her expensive new tires. The confrontation that follows challenges her, enlightens him, and unites both in a dramatic conclusion.

THE RETENTION OF HUMANITY

1.

(Despite his wealth, age, and the hectic pace of his business activities, *he had somehow retained a youthful vigor for fun and frolic and this is what had attracted her in the first place.*)

2.

(Though she now had access to a limousine and had charge accounts at his expense in the best stores in New York, *she remained at heart the same country girl she had been on the day of her arrival from Kentucky.*)

3.

(While she continued to drive her silver Lincoln, *she had no use for her furs and expensive jewelry.*)

4.

(There was no need for her to work, *but her active mind refused to adapt to such a state of affairs and she didn't like feeling dependent on her boyfriend*—not because he would think less of her *but because she would think less of herself.*)

5.

(Brought into the organization as a junior executive, she had quickly demonstrated to many skeptical senior executives an astute mind and mature disposition, an ability and desire to learn *without ever expecting or wanting special treatment as the boss's girlfriend.*)

6.

(Her move to New York and her rapid rise in the organization *in no way detracted from her close ties to her parents, back in Kentucky, whom she continued to telephone every weekend and to visit on holidays* not out of a sense of obligation *but affection.*)

## CHARLIE WATTS: MADRID MEXICO CITY MONTEVIDEO

*Mick Jagger and Texas-born girlfriend Jerry Hall, escaping from the mad social whirl of the Stones' current American tour, are believed to be weekending at a friend's place on Montauk Point. Jagger, guest of Princess Grace, while attending the opening of the second annual circus festival in the Principality of Monaco*
*during a party in the five-story 18th-century Landau-Bain*
*where he stopped into a local record shack in Kingston's*
*vacationing in Norway, took Liv Ullman to dinner in*
*says that if he did half the things the magazines say*
*inaugurated a floating casino in Manila Bay*
*and, friends think, still carries a torch for*
*during the champagne and canapé service*
*flown in for the event on their private jet*
*yet a wonderful father to daughter Jade*
*with the Empress Farah Diba of Iran*
*kept the music going until after 2:30*
*in Linda Ronstadt's Malibu home*
*yet maintains a strict regimen*
*showering acquaintances with*
*visiting designer Thea Porter*
*took Farrah Fawcett-Majors*
*at the wheel of his BMW*
*the birthday party for*
*at a New York inspot*
*in a gold lamé jacket*
*took Cheryl Tiegs*
*seen leaving with*
*near St. Moritz*
*looking terrific*
*rumored to be*
*Andy Warhol*
*peasant soup*
*Angie Bowie*

*weekending*
*on his arm*
*Studio 54*
*attending*
*rumored*
*escorted*
*guest of*
*Bel Air*
*Malibu*
*Bianca*
*going*
*seen*
*who*
*yet*
*in*
*at*

At precisely 1:27 yesterday morning a man believed to be Mick Jagger was seen climbing down a fire escape in Harlem. He dropped to the pavement just below, then stepped swiftly to the curb where a chauffeured limousine, its headlights dimmed, its motor idling, was waiting to speed him away. A soft rain was falling, the wet streets were deserted—not a light shone in a window anywhere.

## APRIL IN OHIO (OHIO, APRIL IN)

In April, in Ohio, the forest yields a white-tailed deer, timid, soft, stepping out onto the still frozen gray ground, cautious in the brittle dream-light of a tentative spring.

In Ohio, in the morning, the scent of grass, freshly mown, hangs pleasantly in the air above baseball diamonds.

In April, in Ohio, *Dawn of the Dead* opens in the cities, all around the suburbs, and at the drive-ins in the countryside where the wind in the evening stirs the slowly awakening forest.

In April, at dusk, people water their lawns with green hoses in the shady suburbs of Columbus.

In April, in Cincinnati, the baseball season gets underway. With a shout the players jump out of the dugout and jog across the soft green field. But behind home plate the catcher, with the sweetest smile of all, crouches and nervously pounds his fist in his mitt.

In the evening, in Columbus, at the Raintree, the Forum, and the Twin 1 drive-in on Harrisburg Pike, where the wind sighs through the trees, and the clouds, billowing in the moonlight, ride the April dark—

In Ohio, in April, where everything smells so fragrant at sunrise—

In April, at noon, when Cleveland has the Cleveland Indians—

In April, in Ohio, a man driving home on the turnpike in the evening, tired, listening to the radio, anxious to get back and prepare a simple dinner, glances up, as usual, as he passes the gigantic outdoor screen—but slows down just perceptibly as the dead, with that uninhabited look in their eyes, stumble out of the bare woods and shamble across the still soft green meadows.

In April, at dusk, the puddles glimmer quietly on the sidewalks and in the driveways.

In April, at dusk, the green hoses lie coiled nastily on the freshly mown lawns.

## VOCABULARY EXERCISE

1.

Pentagon officials have gone on the offensive against their critics in the State Department, arguing that the South African naval base at Simonstown—the only adequately equipped naval base in the Southern Hemisphere between South America and Australia—contributes directly to the protection of the strategic Cape of Good Hope which 2,270 oil tankers pass each month.

2.

Conservative forces in the Senate have been quick to remind the President of the strategic value of the Panama Canal whose 533 square-mile canal zone with its own U.S. schools, post offices, and courts, will soon be turned over to a government whose political—

3.

An overriding sense of trouble—a foreboding that Turkey may be heading into unsurmountable difficulties—is gripping this strategically located country that anchors the southern flank of NATO and borders the Soviet—

4.

Shaba, whose rich deposits of copper, cobalt, and other minerals provide about 60 per cent of Zaire's foreign exchange, is threatened by Angolan-trained rebels harbored in the strategic border area of—

5.

The troubles in oil-rich South Yemen, which overlooks the strategic Babal Mandela Strait, the channel through which all Red Sea traffic must pass on its way to the Indian Ocean—

6.

Although Iceland has no army or navy, its strategic location along the major northern shipping lanes has made it a vital link in Western Europe's—

7.

The Azores, strategically situated in the North Atlantic, midway between the United States and Western—

8.

Japan, strategically located next to two giants—China and the USSR—is worried that—

9.

The strategic U.S. Navy base on Diego Garcia island in the Indian—

10.

The strategic hamlet of Tu Chung—

## ACCESSORY AFTER THE FACT

In the morning the man, who looked like any successful businessman, strolled unhurriedly into the main post office and picked up a small packet that had arrived just after midnight from Zurich, Switzerland.

Anyone following him in those days would not have been surprised at the taverns and restaurants he frequented. Certainly no waiter could have mistaken the soft-spoken, refined New Englander sipping wine and gazing at the lunch hour traffic for anything other than a contented executive.

To other clients he might have been an elegant Bostonian gentleman in a three-piece suit trying out a hunting rifle in one of New England's better sporting shops.

It was a white colonial house in the older part of the suburbs—nothing overly ornate from the outside view, and certainly nothing to cause it to stand out from the other irregularly placed estates on the leafy street.

The sun had just begun to go down when the black sedan—no one watching it pass would have thought twice about it—pulled slowly through the marble gateway, the driver pausing briefly on a rise in the driveway.

The scene that greeted him through the open door could have been any gathering of successful industrialists, relaxing in the atmosphere of a private club.

The man, who looked like any man—

LINES

Everytime I opened my mouth—another poet's swallows would fly out.
Everytime I uncapped my pen—another writer's marigolds would burst into bloom.

Finally, well-meaning friends persuaded me
the whole problem could be reduced to
the problem of
*the line*
so I set myself to clear things up.

I thought of the smuggler who, with the aid of his compass, follows the border line through the tropical rain forest at night;
of the clergyman who, shouting from his pulpit, draws the line between good and evil;
of the New England stadium where, beneath bright autumn skies, the players pile up on the scrimmage line;
and of the aging athlete who, in the same stadium, after the peanut vendor has passed without recognition, delicately traces with the tips of his fingers the first lines of sorrow in his once smooth forehead.

Still, this had little to do with me.
I decided to broaden my search.

I remembered my father who used to say that only the hit man's line on the third race in the sixth form could always be depended upon;
the diplomat whose immunity briefcase was almost always lined with heroin;
the newspaper baron who, after his child had been kidnapped, pleaded to keep "all lines of communication open," though he never did in his papers;
the unemployed shoemaker who, crouching on the gravelly

roof, fixed the ruler's forehead in his line of sight;
and the ruler who, having survived an assassination attempt, then adopted a hard line:

*and this is a line that rules out all other lines,*
*this is a line that rules out all other lines.*

Then again, I was told my job would be easier
if I restricted my search to literary concerns.

I turned on the TV and sure enough, on the evening talk show the best selling author was speaking so unabashedly about his new historical novel on heroic lines that he was a genuine pleasure to watch;
then at a small literary function the next night the evening's honored writer was shouting, "Such subject matter is not in my line, such subject matter is not in my line," to loud, and slightly too long, applause;
and then I recalled that some years before his death John Berryman had written of a poem of his, "Its form comprises eighteen-line sections, three six-line stanzas, each normally (for feet) 5-5-3-5-5-3 . . ."

But all this only increased my sense of suffocation
and made me want to shake my fist and shout,
*"Don't give me any of your lines,*
*I don't want any of your lines."*
Instead I got my umbrella and went out.

When I am feeling grumpy I growl at the old woman who sneaks ahead of me in the long checkout line in the supermarket.
When I am tired I wait in line with the other tired ones to punch the clock at the end of the day.
When I am anxious for the weekend to begin I stand in the bank line on Friday afternoon with the other ones anxious for the weekend to begin.
And when Saturday night comes around and I find myself once again at a loss I stand in line in the pouring rain waiting outside the cinema.

When I am lacking confidence in myself I write poems whose form comprises eighteen-line sections, three six-line stanzas, each normally (for feet) 5-5-3-5-5-3 . . .
When I am worried what the others will think I avoid subjects that are not in line with what I know the others expect.
When I am frightened—I stay in line.

When evening comes around and I feel at a loss I stand in line in the pouring rain waiting outside the cinema.
When evening comes around, for want of anything better to do, I stand in line in the pouring rain waiting outside the cinema.
When evening comes around, *as a last resort,* I stand in line in the pouring rain waiting outside the cinema.

And now the line begins to move,—
and now the rain drums lightly on the moving umbrellas.

## SPAGHETTI WESTERN TITLES

*A Bullet For the General*
*Dead or Alive*
*Death Rides A Horse*
*The Dirty Story of the West*
**Django*
*Django Always Draws Second*
*Django and Sartana Are Coming*
*Django Defies Sartana*
*Django Does Not Forgive*
*Django, Get a Coffin Ready*
*Django, Kill*
*Django Shoots First*
*Django the Bastard*
*Django the Condemned*
*Don't Wait For Django, Shoot*
*A Few Dollars For Django*
*Find a Place To Die*
*A Fistful of Dollars*
*A Fistful of Dynamite*
*For a Dollar in the Teeth*
*For a Few Dollars Less*
*For a Few Dollars More*
*God Forgives, I Don't*
*The Good, the Bad, and the Ugly*
*Gunfight at Red Sands*
*Guns of Violence*
*The Handsome, the Ugly, and the Stupid*
*The Hills Run Red*
*I Go, I Shoot, and I Return*
*Light the Fuse, Sartana's Coming*
*Long Live Death . . . Preferably Yours*
*My Name is Nobody*

*Watched by Jimmy Cliff at the Kingston Rialto in *The Harder They Come.*

*No Room To Die*
*Once Upon a Time in the West*
*100,000 Dollars For Ringo*
*A Pistol For Ringo*
*Pistols Don't Argue*
*A Professional Gun*
*The Return of Django*
*The Return of Ringo*
*Ringo Against Everyone*
*Ringo's Two Sons*
*Samson and the Treasure of the Incas*
*Sartana, If Your Left Arm Offends, Cut It Off*
*Sartana Kills Them All*
*Sartana's Coming*
*Sartana the Grave-Digger*
*Sartana Will Pay (Have a Good Funeral)*
*Son of Django*
*10,000 Dollars Blood Money*
*They Call Him Holy Spirit*
*They Call Me Providence*
*They Call Me Trinity*
*Today It's Me, Tomorrow You*
*Trinity is Still My Name*
*Trinity Sees Red*
*Viva Django*

## AUTUMN LEAVES

Whenever it is dusk and a sudden gust of wind sends leaves whirling and skittering across the pavement—

Whenever it is evening and a swollen black plastic trash bag, knotted at the top, sits in an autumn driveway while a rake leans quietly against the nearby tree—

But then when, a short while later, returning from the grocery store you pass the same driveway and glance through the bedroom window and notice the same swollen black plastic trash bag sitting heavily in the center of someone's sagging bed—

And then when the same swollen black plastic trash bag appears in the back of a mysterious station wagon that has been left parked on a side street and it is almost midnight—

And then when you take a walk early the next morning down by the river near the old abandoned sawmill and spot the black plastic trash bag half-hidden in a tangle of bushes—

And when by noon you have worked up your nerve and step *closer* to the swollen black plastic bag—

And when by midafternoon you have actually leaned over and *touched* the swollen black plastic trash bag—

And when by late afternoon you have actually *given up* trying to unknot the top of the hideously swollen black plastic trash bag and instead slash it open with a knife—

Then: The next time it is dusk and a sudden gust of wind sends leaves whirling and skittering across the pavement—

## UNFREE ASSOCIATIONS

*For Reggie Jackson and Andreas Baader,*
*October 18, 1977*

In the stadium one bright, fall morning
when Willie Mays stepped to the plate
everyone rose from the seats as one
—there was poetry in the way he held the bat—
and with the Giants and Yankees tied for the series
and a tie score in the top of the ninth
the whole world seemed to hang in the balance—

Stretching around the curvature of the outfield wall
the advertising posters flashed in the sunshine
while in center field Mickey Mantle
fanned himself with his cap.
It was very quiet in the stadium,
there was a full count,
and when Whitey Ford went into his wind-up
I squeezed my father's hand.
*Crack!*—Mantle drifted back,
then broke into a run
but when he dove for the ball
he slipped, slamming up against the wall:
above him, a poster—*Capri, the Sexy European*
A woman sat on the hood of the car
with such aplomb I found it unnerving,
and even as Mantle leaped up to chase the ball
which had ricocheted off the wall
I couldn't tear my eyes from the poster.

Years later
while driving my Capri to work at dawn
a billboard rose before me,
a two-hundred pound football star,
in helmet and shoulder pads
—there was poetry in the way he held the toothpaste—

and when I looked out at the pine trees that landscaped the freeway,
their tops tossing in the early morning wind,
I was overcome by a sudden surge of emotion
and wanted to break open the cellophane on a new pack of anything,
then roll down my window and take a deep breath—

In my capacity as copywriter it was my duty
to try and rescue the secret but logical connections
between objects and the feelings they evoked,
to try to make life itself
more and more evocative.

But in the years that followed
more and more
wherever I went
something would remind me of something else—
And though it only seemed natural to glance at the long glass rows of bottles in a liquor store window and think of pine trees mounting a snowy mountain slope—
Or to hear someone in the next room smoothing out a sheet of Alcoa aluminum foil and suddenly feel transported to a long white Caribbean beach with surf crashing all along it—
Still
after each storm
I would find myself searching the changing skies for the comforting yellow arches of McDonald's—
And whenever I passed a Woolworth's,
whenever I would see the bubble gum machine out front
—the round glass case filled with bright-colored balls—
I would suddenly long for the din of a big city playground,
the downcourt dribbling of basketballs,
the jangling of backboards—
and then the last cries at dusk.

In this way
as the years went by
the time and space of my world grew strange
until the whole world seemed to ache
and everytime the sun went down
it seemed to pull part of the horizon down with it.

And once when I dropped a tube of haircream on the bathroom tiles and it bounced, I thought—companionship.
When I left the carton of ice cream sitting on the table and returned later to find it hadn't melted—integrity.
My supermarket purchases in the big crisp bag—an autumn lane, a pumpkin stand.
The plastic yellow shower curtain in all its shimmering radiance—school children hurrying home in the rain.
Yes, and the new red blender on the formica counter—my father taking me after dinner to the snowy lot behind the housing project to help pick out a Christmas tree.
Then again, on a winter night through a frosted window the blue glow of a tv screen—the fear is settling into the streets, the world is coming home.

## ETHNIC SLUR

1.

(It begins at dawn with a fruitcart peddler.)

2.

(Lucky Luciano / Tom Gagliano / Joseph Bonnano / Vincent Mangano / Carlo Gambino / Stefano Magaddino / Angelo Bruno / Gennero Angiulo / Tony Accardo / Frank Zito / Carlos Marcello / James Civello)

3.

(The birthday cake was so large they had to laugh. "Why it's big enough to contain a machine gun nest!")

4.

(A steel drum filled with cement at the bottom of the Harlem River.)

5.

("Frankie was a peaceful guy, a diplomat.")

6.

(Albert Anastasia / Giuseppe Masseria / Raymond Patriarca / Joseph Ida / James Lanza / Sam Giancana / Philip Bruccola / Jerry Catena / Natale Euola / Joseph Modica / Vincenti Teresa / Paul Sciacca / Charles Panarella)

7.

("Wot's a matter? Ya got carburetor trouble?")

8.

(Said Lucky on handing the contract for Dutch Schultz to Lepke Buchalter: "Let their own *take care of their own.*")

9.

(sun-wrinkled old men knocking olive trees with long poles)

10.

(It ends at dusk on a balcony above the sea.)

## BEFORE IT GROWS DARK

Were you thinking of the barn-red covered bridge
at the moment the first snows began to fall?

Were you thinking of how the thin mist rises
from the ghostly marsh at dawn?

What exactly was it you were thinking of? Ice crystals
in the frozen mud? the vines clinging to the half-dead
black cherry tree? how slowly the dusk seeped
from the blue coniferous forest that surrounded
your cottage?

*No one cares what you're thinking.*

You who lament

"the last literary generation"

"the loss of the authority of culture"

"the end of the logic of tradition"

After the last leaves have fallen—

After all the cows have gone home—

After the last gray embers have collapsed
on the last ridiculous hearth—

After you've taken your last walk
through the last shattered, stinking hills—

*Look at those black storm clouds!*

All of you is so much alike
and everything you say is not funny.

MICHAEL COVINO was born in Brooklyn in 1950, raised in the Bronx, and attended the State University of New York at Stony Brook and the University of California, Berkeley. His short stories have appeared in *Carolina Quarterly, Chelsea, Chicago Review, The North American Review,* and elsewhere, and in 1982 he received a National Endowment for the Arts grant in fiction. He lives in Berkeley, where he writes a film column for *The East Bay Express.*

*Unfree Associations* is his first collection of poems. The poems were written between 1977 and 1981.

## Books from the Berkeley Poets Workshop & Press

*Berkeley Poets Cooperative Anthology*, 1970-1980, poetry & fiction, 256 pages, $6.95

*Snake Blossoms* by Belden, poetry & fiction, 64 pages, $3.00

*Jackbird* by Bruce Boston, fiction, 88 pages, $3.00

*She Comes When You're Leaving* by Bruce Boston, fiction, 62 pages, $3.95

*Slow Juggling* by Karen Brodine, poetry, 48 pages, $3.00

*Seaward* by Betty Coon, poetry, 44 pages, $3.00

*Newspaper Stories* by Patricia Dienstfrey, poetry, 36 pages, $3.75

*All Pieces of a Legacy* by Charles Entrekin, poetry & fiction, 54 pages, $3.00

*Casting for the Cutthroat* by Charles Entrekin, poetry, 48 pages, $3.95

*Half a Bottle of Catsup* by Ted Fleischman, poetry, 40 pages, $3.00

*Wordrows* by Bruce Hawkins, poetry, 40 pages, $3.00

*The Ghost of the Buick* by Bruce Hawkins, poetry, 48 pages, $3.95

*Wash Me on Home, Mama* by Peter Najarian, fiction, 84 pages, $3.50

*Once More Out of Darkness* by Alicia Ostriker, poetry, 32 pages, $3.00

*The Machine Shuts Down* by Rod Tulloss, poetry, 40 pages, $3.95

*John Danced* by Gail Rudd, poetry, 40 pages, $4.00

Forthcoming: *Self-Portrait With Hand Microscope* by Lucille Day, poetry, 48 pages, $3.95; *Hear My Story* by Dennis Folly, poetry, 48 pages, $3.95.